SUPERPOWER SCIENCE

FANTASTIC FORCES AND MOTION

JOY LIN

ILLUSTRATED BY ALAN BROWN

B.E.S.
PUBLISHING

FIRST EDITION FOR THE UNITED STATES, ITS
TERRITORIES AND DEPENDENCIES, THE PHILIPPINE
REPUBLIC, AND CANADA PUBLISHED IN 2019 BY
B.E.S. PUBLISHING CO.

TEXT COPYRIGHT © JOY LIN, 2018
ART AND DESIGN COPYRIGHT © HODDER & STOUGHTON, 2018
FIRST PUBLISHED IN GREAT BRITAIN IN 2018 BY
WAYLAND, AN IMPRINT OF HACHETTE CHILDREN'S
GROUP, PART OF HODDER & STOUGHTON.

ALL INQUIRIES SHOULD BE ADDRESSED TO:
B.E.S. PUBLISHING CO.
250 WIRELESS BOULEVARD
HAUPPAUGE, NY 11788
WWW.BES-PUBLISHING.COM

ISBN: 978-1-4380-1265-0

LIBRARY OF CONGRESS CONTROL NUMBER: 2018951832

DATE OF MANUFACTURE: JANUARY 2019
MANUFACTURED BY: WKT, SHENZHEN, CHINA

PRINTED IN CHINA
9 8 7 6 5 4 3 2 1

What if I had a superpower?

HAVEN'T WE ALL ASKED OURSELVES THIS QUESTION AT SOME POINT? IT WOULD BE AMAZING TO BE ABLE TO FLY OR RUN SUPER FAST; MANIPULATE TIME OR BE SUPER STRONG. ARE THESE ABILITIES THE STUFF OF DREAMS OR WILL WE ONE DAY BE ABLE TO BE REAL-LIFE SUPERHEROES?

ONCE UPON A TIME WE WERE ONLY ABLE TO OBSERVE THE STARS FROM EARTH AND DREAM OF EXPLORING SPACE, THEN ONE DAY, WE SENT MEN TO THE MOON! SCIENCE IS DEFINITELY CATCHING UP WITH OUR IMAGINATIONS. LET'S SEE WHAT HAPPENS WHEN YOU APPLY THE LAWS OF SCIENCE TO SUPERPOWERS...

CONTENTS

WHAT ARE FORCES AND MOTION?

First, let's look at the science.

WERE YOU TOLD THAT THE 17TH-CENTURY SCIENTIST ISAAC NEWTON (1642–1727) ONLY CAME UP WITH THE LAW OF GRAVITY BECAUSE HE WAS HIT ON THE HEAD BY A FALLING APPLE? AS FAMOUS AS THAT STORY IS, IT DIDN'T REALLY HAPPEN. THERE WAS A TREE WITH APPLES, WHICH HELPED HIM COME UP WITH THE FUNDAMENTAL LAWS OF FORCES AND MOTION, THOUGH.

FIRST LAW OF MOTION

NEWTON'S FIRST LAW OF MOTION IS CALLED "THE LAW OF INERTIA." IT STATES THAT AN UNMOVING OBJECT WILL STAY STILL UNTIL A FORCE (A PUSH OR PULL ACTING ON THE OBJECT) ACTS UPON IT. SO A BOOK THAT IS RESTING ON THE TABLE IS NOT GOING TO MOVE UNLESS SOMEBODY MOVES IT OR THE TABLE COLLAPSES UNDERNEATH IT.

THE LAW OF INERTIA ALSO STATES THAT AN OBJECT IN MOTION WILL STAY IN MOTION WITH THE SAME VELOCITY (SPEED IN A PARTICULAR DIRECTION) UNTIL A FORCE ACTS UPON IT. SO IF YOU WERE TO SLIDE THAT BOOK OVER TO YOUR FRIEND, IT SHOULD KEEP GOING UNTIL SOMETHING OR SOMEONE STOPS IT.

THAT CAN'T BE RIGHT. WE ALL KNOW THE BOOK WILL EVENTUALLY STOP EVEN IF NOBODY IS THERE TO CATCH IT. NO MATTER HOW LONG THE TABLE IS...

IN REALITY, A FORCE CALLED FRICTION ACTS AGAINST THE BOOK, AND GRADUALLY STOPS IT FROM MOVING. FRICTION IS A FORCE THAT SLOWS DOWN OR STOPS OBJECTS WHEN THEY SLIDE, SCRAPE, OR RUB AGAINST EACH OTHER.

SECOND LAW OF MOTION

IN NEWTON'S SECOND LAW OF MOTION, THERE ARE THREE RELATIONSHIPS: ❶ FORCE (THE PULL AND PUSH) AND MASS (HOW HEAVY SOMETHING IS), ❷ MASS AND ACCELERATION (AN INCREASE IN SPEED), AND ❸ FORCE AND ACCELERATION. THESE THREE RELATIONSHIPS TRANSLATE TO:

1. THE HEAVIER THE OBJECT IS, THE MORE FORCE IT TAKES TO MOVE IT.

2. WITH THE SAME FORCE, YOU CAN GIVE A LIGHT OBJECT MORE ACCELERATION THAN YOU CAN A HEAVY OBJECT.

3. THE MORE FORCE YOU USE, THE MORE ACCELERATION YOU GIVE TO THE OBJECT.

THIRD LAW OF MOTION

NEWTON'S THIRD LAW OF MOTION STATES THAT FOR EVERY ACTION, THERE IS AN EQUAL AND OPPOSITE REACTION.

MASS IS ACTED ON BY GRAVITY (THE FORCE THAT PULLS OBJECTS TOWARD EACH OTHER). GRAVITY PRESSES ON WHATEVER SURFACE AN OBJECT IS PLACED ON, SUCH AS A BOOK ON A DESK. THE BOOK IS PUSHING AGAINST THE DESK AND THE DESK IS PUSHING BACK AGAINST THE BOOK. THE BOOK DOESN'T MOVE BECAUSE THE FORCES ARE BALANCED.

SO WHEN YOU ARE STANDING ON A STAIR, YOU'RE EXERTING FORCE ON THE STAIR, BUT THE STAIR IS ALSO PUSHING UP WITH THE SAME AMOUNT OF FORCE.

IF THE STAIR IS NOT STURDY ENOUGH TO SUPPORT YOUR WEIGHT, GUESS WHAT HAPPENS? YOU FALL THROUGH IT!

Now let's see what happens when we apply the three laws of motion to superpowers.

THE SILVER SWIFT: SHE'S A HIGH-FLYER!

Wouldn't it be amazing if you could fly? You could save someone stuck at the top of a high mountain...

HELP!

OR DODGE TRAFFIC IN RUSH HOUR AND NEVER BE LATE FOR SCHOOL.

BETTER STILL, YOU COULD HAVE A BIRD'S-EYE VIEW OF YOUR TOWN AND SPOT ANY CRIME!

BUT HOW HIGH WOULD YOU FLY? IT WOULD MAKE SENSE TO FLY ONLY A FEW FLOORS UP SO YOU COULD STILL SEE ALL THE ROAD SIGNS AND BUILDINGS IN ORDER TO NAVIGATE AND SWOOP DOWN QUICKLY TO STOP CRIME. WELL, THERE ARE SEVERAL PROBLEMS WITH THAT.

THE SILVER SWIFT'S SUPERPOWERS
- to fly high up in the sky
- to have a bird's-eye view of the world
- to rescue people in high places

FIRST OF ALL, YOU NEED TO WATCH OUT FOR BIRDS, ELECTRICAL WIRES, AND ALL THOSE ROAD SIGNS.

OKAY, WE'LL GIVE YOU A HELMET TO STOP YOU FROM BANGING YOUR HEAD. STILL, WHEN YOU FLY THROUGH A SWARM OF INSECTS, YOU'RE GOING TO HAVE TO PULL OVER AND BRUSH THEM AWAY FROM YOUR FACE.

YUK!

YOU KNOW WHAT ELSE YOU HAVE TO DODGE? BUILDINGS!

THUD!

SINCE FLYING ONLY A FEW FLOORS FROM THE GROUND IS TOO HAZARDOUS, WHAT IF YOU WERE TO FLY HIGHER UP IN THE SKY?

WELL, THE HIGHER YOU GO, THE LOWER THE AIR PRESSURE BECOMES. AIR PRESSURE IS THE PUSHING FORCE OF AIR MOLECULES. THE PRESSURE DECREASES AS YOU GO HIGHER BECAUSE THERE ARE FEWER MOLECULES IN THE AIR. THIS AFFECTS THE TEMPERATURE, WHICH ALSO GOES DOWN. SO LAYER UP, IT'S GOING TO BE A COLD RIDE!

YOU MIGHT NOT THINK BEING A LITTLE CHILLY IS A BIG DEAL, BUT AT A JET PLANE'S TYPICAL ALTITUDE OF 30,000 FT (10,000 M), THE OUTSIDE TEMPERATURE IS APPROXIMATELY -60°F (-50°C). THAT'S 90 DEGREES COLDER THAN WATER'S FREEZING POINT!

AT SUCH EXTREME TEMPERATURES, YOUR EXPOSED SKIN WOULD BECOME PUFFY AND CRACK. IF YOU EXPOSE YOUR FINGERS AND TOES TO THE COLD FOR TOO LONG, FROSTBITE CAN OCCUR, WHICH IS WHEN YOUR SKIN AND TISSUES FREEZE AND SOMETIMES FALL OFF. YOU WOULDN'T WANT TO LOSE ANY FINGERS OR TOES, WOULD YOU?

IT'S CCCCCOLD!!!

EVEN WORSE, ALL IT TAKES IS FOR YOUR CORE BODY TEMPERATURE TO DROP TWO DEGREES FOR HYPOTHERMIA (A CONDITION OF DANGEROUSLY LOW BODY TEMPERATURE) TO START KICKING IN. THIS GRADUALLY LEADS TO SHIVERING, MENTAL CONFUSION, DIFFICULTY SPEAKING, MAJOR ORGANS FAILING, AND EVENTUALLY...DEATH!

ANOTHER CONSEQUENCE OF THE LOW PRESSURE IS THE EXPANSION OF AIR VOLUME, WHICH MEANS THERE ARE FEWER AIR MOLECULES. SO WHEN YOU BREATHE IN A LUNGFUL OF AIR, THERE IS LESS OXYGEN IN IT! YOU'D NEVER BE ABLE TO BREATHE IN QUICKLY ENOUGH TO MAKE UP FOR IT. QUITE INCONVENIENT SINCE HUMAN BEINGS NEED OXYGEN TO SURVIVE.

OKAY, SO NOW YOU ARE DRESSED WARMLY, WITH A HELMET, AND AN OXYGEN TANK TO HELP YOU BREATHE HIGH IN THE SKY. NOT THE MOST IMPRESSIVE SUPERHERO LOOK ...

A WORD OF WARNING: DON'T FLY STRAIGHT UP! IT MAY LOOK COOL WHEN OTHER SUPERHEROES DO IT, BUT BUBBLES WILL FORM IN YOUR BLOOD AND OTHER PARTS OF YOUR BODY BECAUSE THE PRESSURE AROUND YOU IS DECREASING TOO QUICKLY. THESE BUBBLES WILL EITHER BLOCK THE FLOW OF BLOOD AND STARVE PARTS OF YOUR BODY OF OXYGEN, OR THEY WILL CAUSE DAMAGE BY STRETCHING, TEARING, OR PRESSING ON THE AFFECTED PARTS. IN EXTREME CASES, IT COULD KILL YOU!

Blood cells

Air bubble

Vein

THIS IS WHY DEEP-SEA SCUBA DIVERS ARE TOLD TO COME UP TO THE SURFACE SLOWLY, SO THEY DON'T EXPERIENCE DECOMPRESSION SICKNESS, COMMONLY KNOWN AS "THE BENDS."

ANOTHER THING TO CONSIDER: HOW FAST WOULD YOU BE FLYING? REMEMBER NEWTON'S THIRD LAW OF MOTION? FOR EVERY ACTION, THERE MUST BE AN EQUAL AND OPPOSITE REACTION.

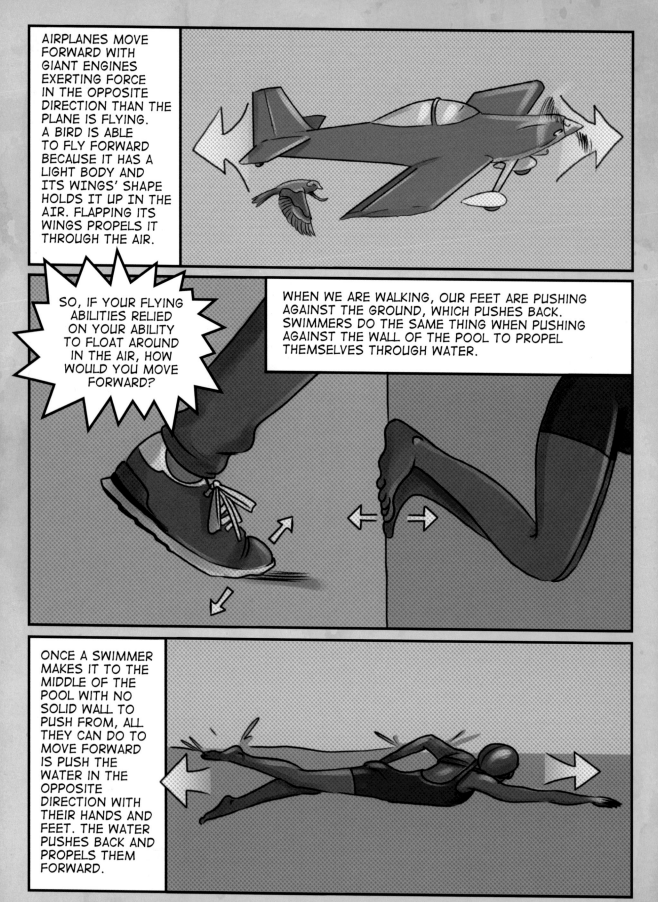

AIRPLANES MOVE FORWARD WITH GIANT ENGINES EXERTING FORCE IN THE OPPOSITE DIRECTION THAN THE PLANE IS FLYING. A BIRD IS ABLE TO FLY FORWARD BECAUSE IT HAS A LIGHT BODY AND ITS WINGS' SHAPE HOLDS IT UP IN THE AIR. FLAPPING ITS WINGS PROPELS IT THROUGH THE AIR.

SO, IF YOUR FLYING ABILITIES RELIED ON YOUR ABILITY TO FLOAT AROUND IN THE AIR, HOW WOULD YOU MOVE FORWARD?

WHEN WE ARE WALKING, OUR FEET ARE PUSHING AGAINST THE GROUND, WHICH PUSHES BACK. SWIMMERS DO THE SAME THING WHEN PUSHING AGAINST THE WALL OF THE POOL TO PROPEL THEMSELVES THROUGH WATER.

ONCE A SWIMMER MAKES IT TO THE MIDDLE OF THE POOL WITH NO SOLID WALL TO PUSH FROM, ALL THEY CAN DO TO MOVE FORWARD IS PUSH THE WATER IN THE OPPOSITE DIRECTION WITH THEIR HANDS AND FEET. THE WATER PUSHES BACK AND PROPELS THEM FORWARD.

THE FASTEST SWIMMER IN RECORDED HISTORY ONLY SWIMS AS FAST AS A NORMAL HUMAN WALKS. THAT'S JUST 5 MPH (8 KPH)! SO, IF YOU WERE TO FLOAT AND PROPEL YOURSELF THROUGH AIR LIKE A SWIMMER THROUGH WATER, FIRST YOU WOULD LOOK VERY UN-SUPERHERO-LIKE SWIMMING IN MIDAIR AND SECOND, WATER AND AIR ARE VERY DIFFERENT SUBSTANCES. YOU WOULD NEED TO PUSH A LOT MORE AIR BACKWARD TO BE ABLE TO MOVE FORWARD.

HAVE YOU EVER SEEN ASTRONAUTS FLOATING AROUND THE INTERNATIONAL SPACE STATION? THEY USE HANDLES ON WALLS AND CEILINGS TO PULL THEMSELVES FORWARD. "SWIMMING" THROUGH AIR JUST ISN'T A PRACTICAL MODE OF TRANSPORTATION.

WE MAY NEVER BE ABLE TO FLY UNAIDED, BUT ADVANCES IN SCIENCE AND TECHNOLOGY HAVE MADE FLIGHT A REALITY WHEN NOT SO LONG AGO IT WAS STILL A FANTASY.

WE STARTED WITH KITES IN CHINA, THEN HOT AIR BALLOONS IN FRANCE, THEN WE MOVED ON TO AIRPLANES AND HELICOPTERS, WHICH NOW CONSTANTLY FLY OVER OUR HEADS. BUT WHAT MOST RESEMBLES SUPERHERO-LIKE FLIGHT ARE JET PACKS. THERE HAVE BEEN ALL SORTS OF DEVELOPMENTS ON THAT FRONT. IN 2017, THE AEROSPACE COMPANY BOEING LAUNCHED A $2-MILLION COMPETITION WITH THE AIM OF MAKING JET PACKS A REALITY BY 2019. FLYING SUPERHEROES MAY VERY WELL BE ZOOMING AROUND YOUR NEIGHBORHOOD SOONER THAN YOU THINK!

THE ACCELERATOR:
CATCH HIM IF YOU CAN!

What if you could move with incredible super speed like the peregrine falcon, the fastest animal in the world? You would never be late for anything!

SINCE THE PEREGRINE FALCON CAN REACH SPEEDS OF OVER 200 MPH (300 KPH), YOU'D BE ABLE TO CATCH ANY BAD GUYS IN A HIGH-SPEED CAR CHASE!

OR EVEN PUSH SOMEONE OUT OF THE WAY OF A FASTBALL (A FAST BASEBALL)!

THE FASTEST THROW EVER RECORDED WAS AROUND 100 MPH (170 KPH), WHICH IS HIGHER THAN THE SPEED LIMIT ON THE FASTEST ROADS. IT WOULD HURT A LOT TO BE HIT BY A FASTBALL, BUT WHAT OTHER CONSEQUENCES WOULD OCCUR?

THE ACCELERATOR'S SUPERPOWERS
- to move as fast as the speediest animal, the peregrine falcon
- to win high-speed chases
- to never be late for anything

WHEN THE GIRL IS STANDING THERE, HER SPEED IS ZERO. WHEN YOU PUSH HER AT THE SPEED OF A PEREGRINE FALCON, HER SPEED BECOMES 200 MPH (300 KPH). THAT IS A DRASTIC CHANGE IN A MATTER OF A SECOND.

REMEMBER NEWTON'S SECOND LAW OF MOTION (SEE PAGE 5)? THE MORE FORCE YOU EXERT ON HER, THE HIGHER THE ACCELERATION AND VICE VERSA. WITH THIS LEVEL OF ACCELERATION, IT MEANS YOU HAVE EXERTED A LOT OF FORCE ON THIS GIRL. HOW MUCH, YOU ASK?

INSTEAD OF LETTING HER GET HIT AT 100 MPH (170 KPH) BY A BASEBALL THAT WEIGHS 0.3 LB (0.15 KG), YOU JUST CRASHED INTO HER AT A MUCH HIGHER SPEED. EXCEPT YOUR MASS IS PROBABLY SOMETHING LIKE MORE THAN 200 TIMES AS MUCH AS THE BASEBALL, EXERTING MORE THAN 200 TIMES AS MUCH FORCE ON THIS POOR GIRL.

REMEMBER NEWTON'S FIRST LAW OF MOTION (SEE PAGE 4)? THE LAW OF INERTIA STATES THAT AN OBJECT AT REST WILL STAY AT REST UNTIL AN UNBALANCED FORCE ACTS UPON IT. SO IF YOU PUSH THIS GIRL TO HER LEFT, ALL OF HER INTERNAL ORGANS WOULD CRASH INTO THE RIGHT SIDE OF HER BODY AND HER BRAIN WOULD CRASH INTO THE RIGHT SIDE OF HER SKULL.

THE LAW OF INERTIA ALSO STATES THAT AN OBJECT IN MOTION WILL STAY IN MOTION UNTIL AN UNBALANCED FORCE ACTS UPON IT. SO, WHEN THIS GIRL IS SUDDENLY STOPPED, ALL OF HER INTERNAL ORGANS WOULD CRASH BACK INTO THE LEFT SIDE OF HER BODY AND HER BRAIN WOULD CRASH INTO THE LEFT SIDE OF HER SKULL.

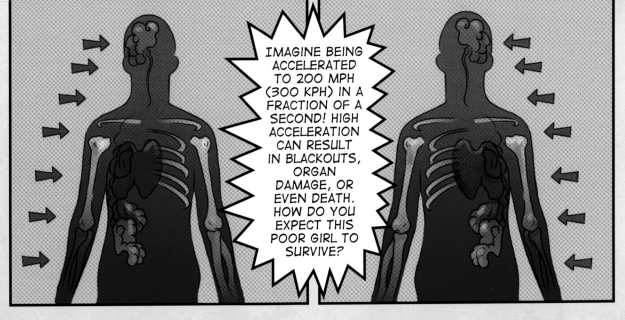

IMAGINE BEING ACCELERATED TO 200 MPH (300 KPH) IN A FRACTION OF A SECOND! HIGH ACCELERATION CAN RESULT IN BLACKOUTS, ORGAN DAMAGE, OR EVEN DEATH. HOW DO YOU EXPECT THIS POOR GIRL TO SURVIVE?

THEORETICALLY SPEAKING, IF YOU CAN'T STOP THE BALL, IT'S BETTER IF YOU JUST LET THE GIRL GET HIT BY THE BALL INSTEAD OF MOVING HER AT SUPER SPEED. YES, YOU CAN ABSOLUTELY GET HER TO THE HOSPITAL BECAUSE IT'S NOT THE SPEED THAT INJURES HER, IT'S THE SUDDEN ACCELERATION AND THE SUDDEN STOP.

HUMANS TRAVEL IN AIRPLANES AT 600 MPH (1,000 KPH) ALL THE TIME AND THAT'S OKAY. AS LONG AS YOU DON'T SPEED UP TOO FAST, SHE CAN SURVIVE TRAVELING AT 186 MPH (300 KPH).

OKAY, SO USING SUPER SPEED TO PUSH PEOPLE OUT OF THE WAY IS NOT VERY PRACTICAL. WHAT IF YOU JUST USE IT TO TRAVEL? FLYING HAS TOO MANY COMPLICATED ISSUES (SEE PAGE 11), SO LET'S DISCUSS RUNNING LIKE THE WIND.

OUCH!

HAVE YOU SEEN THE FRONT BUMPER OF A CAR AFTER A DRIVE IN THE COUNTRYSIDE? IT LOOKS LIKE A GRAVEYARD FOR INSECTS, DOESN'T IT? WELL, PREPARE FOR THE SAME FATE, BUT ON YOUR FACE ...
SEE THAT CHIP IN THE WINDSHIELD FROM A FLYING ROCK PROPELLED BY A PASSING CAR? YOU'LL BE SUBJECTING YOUR BODY TO THOSE DAMAGES, TOO.

EVEN IF THERE ARE NO BIG ROCKS AROUND, AIR IS STILL NOT EMPTY. IT IS FULL OF SMALL PARTICLES AS WELL AS A COMBINATION OF DUST AND SAND ON MOST ROADS.

REMEMBER NEWTON'S THIRD LAW OF MOTION (SEE PAGE 5)? FOR EVERY ACTION, THERE IS AN EQUAL AND OPPOSITE REACTION. IF YOU ARE RUNNING INTO GRAINS OF SAND MORE THAN TWICE AS FAST AS CARS ON FAST ROADS, IT WOULD FEEL AS IF THE GRAINS OF SAND WERE BEING SHOT AT YOU BY A SLINGSHOT.

OKAY, LET'S SAY YOU'RE WEARING A REINFORCED SUIT THAT PROTECTS YOU FROM ALL DEBRIS ON THE ROAD. WHAT ABOUT THE BIGGER STUFF, YOU KNOW, LIKE CARS, BUILDINGS, AND PEOPLE? HOW DO YOU PLAN TO DODGE THEM WHILE TRAVELING AT YOUR SUPERHERO SPEED?

IMAGINE YOU ARE DRIVING A CAR ON A MAIN ROAD AT 60 MPH (95 KPH). A CUTE, FLUFFY BUNNY HOPS OUT IN FRONT OF YOU AND YOU DON'T WANT TO HIT IT. HOW LONG DO YOU THINK IT WOULD TAKE FOR YOUR CAR TO STOP?

FIRST, YOUR EYES WOULD SEE THE BUNNY AND SEND THE VISUAL IMAGE TO THE PART OF YOUR BRAIN THAT PROCESSES SIGHT, THE OCCIPITAL LOBE.

THE INFORMATION IS SENT TO THE PART OF THE BRAIN THAT ANALYZES AND MAKES DECISIONS, THE FRONTAL LOBE, WHICH DECIDES TO SAVE THE BUNNY, AND THEREFORE HIT THE BRAKES.

THE INSTRUCTION TO BRAKE IS PASSED DOWN TO THE PART OF THE BRAIN THAT CONTROLS MOVEMENT, THE MOTOR CORTEX. IT SENDS SIGNALS TO YOUR SPINAL CORD, THE COLUMN OF NERVE CELLS THAT CARRIES MESSAGES FROM YOUR BRAIN TO THE REST OF YOUR BODY.

SPINAL CORD

THE SPINAL CORD THEN TELLS YOUR RIGHT FOOT TO COME OFF THE ACCELERATOR AND STOMP ON THE BRAKE PEDAL.

BEST CASE SCENARIO: YOU SEE THE BUNNY AS SOON AS IT HOPS OUT AND YOU REACT IMMEDIATELY TO IT, BUT IT STILL TAKES APPROXIMATELY 0.25 SECONDS FOR YOUR BODY TO NOTICE THE FLUFFY, CUTE BUNNY AND THEN REACT BY HITTING THE BRAKES.

AT 60 MPH (95 KPH), YOU WOULD HAVE ALREADY TRAVELED OVER 20 FT (6 M) JUST IN THOSE 0.25 SECONDS. DEPENDING ON THE CAR AND HOW MUCH WEIGHT IS IN THE CAR, IT COULD TAKE AN ADDITIONAL 300 FT (90 M) OR SO FOR THE CAR TO COME TO A COMPLETE STOP TO AVOID HITTING THE BUNNY. THAT IS THE LENGTH OF ABOUT 50 MEN, 6 FT (1.8 M) TALL, LYING HEAD TO FOOT.

IF IT TAKES YOU ONE EXTRA SECOND TO NOTICE THE BUNNY, THAT'S AN ADDITIONAL 90 FT (26 M), THE LENGTH OF 15 AVERAGE MEN, FOR THE CAR TO STOP. THIS IS WHY A DRIVER SHOULD NEVER TEXT AND DRIVE BECAUSE THAT ONE EXTRA SECOND OF REACTION TIME COULD MEAN THE DIFFERENCE BETWEEN LIFE OR DEATH FOR SOMEBODY, OR SOME BUNNY.

ALL OF THESE NUMBERS WERE CALCULATED ASSUMING THE CAR WAS TRAVELING AT 60 MPH (95 KPH). WHAT DO YOU THINK THE STOPPING DISTANCE WOULD BE IF YOU WERE TRAVELING AT YOUR SUPERHERO SPEED OF 200 MPH (300 KPH)? BY THE TIME YOU HAD SEEN A BUILDING AND DECIDED TO DODGE IT, YOU WOULD HAVE COLLIDED WITH IT.

I CAN'T STOP!

IN FACT, AT 200 MPH (300 KPH), YOU WOULDN'T BE ABLE TO FIND YOUR WAY ALONG A BUSY STREET BECAUSE THERE WOULD BE TOO MANY IMAGES FOR YOUR EYES TO PROCESS QUICKLY. HAVE YOU EVER NOTICED HOW THE BLADES ON A CEILING FAN BLUR AS IT ROTATES? IN ORDER TO USE SUPER SPEED, YOU WOULD NEED SUPER-FAST PERCEPTION AND SUPER-FAST REACTIONS AS WELL. BUT IN THAT CASE, THEN, NORMAL DAY-TO-DAY LIFE WOULD SEEM INCREDIBLY SLOW AND BORING TO YOU IN COMPARISON BECAUSE OF YOUR CHANGED PERCEPTION OF TIME.

WE MAY NEVER BE ABLE TO RUN AT THE SPEED OF A PEREGRINE FALCON, BUT ATHLETES ARE STILL BREAKING RECORDS. OVER A HUNDRED YEARS AGO, IN 1912, THE RECORD FOR THE 100-M RACE WAS 10.6 SECONDS. ATHLETES HAVE SINCE SHAVED TIME OFF THE RECORD. SINCE 2009, THE RECORD HAS STAYED AT 9.58 SECONDS. THAT'S A WHOLE SECOND LESS THAN IN 1912! WHO KNOWS, THE NEXT FASTEST HUMAN IN THE WORLD MIGHT BE IN TRAINING RIGHT NOW—IT MIGHT EVEN BE YOU...

TIME TWISTER:
TICK ... TOCK

**There is never enough time!
What if you could freeze time...**

... SO YOU'D GET THE PLAYGROUND ALL TO YOURSELF ...

SO YOU COULD STUDY FOR A TEST YOU ARE NOT PREPARED FOR ...

OR SO A CAR DOES NOT HIT YOU WHEN YOU ARE TRYING TO SAVE A BUNNY CAUGHT IN THE HEADLIGHTS?

WELL, THINK AGAIN BECAUSE FREEZING TIME COMES WITH A GREAT DEAL OF CONSEQUENCES!

TIME TWISTER'S SUPERPOWERS
- to freeze time
- to move so fast that time slows down

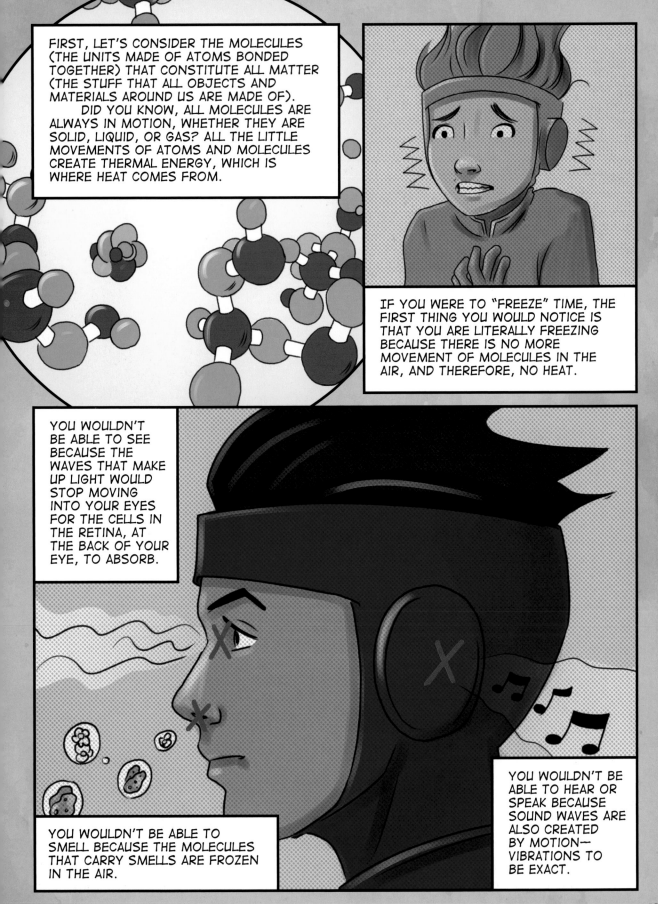

FIRST, LET'S CONSIDER THE MOLECULES (THE UNITS MADE OF ATOMS BONDED TOGETHER) THAT CONSTITUTE ALL MATTER (THE STUFF THAT ALL OBJECTS AND MATERIALS AROUND US ARE MADE OF).

DID YOU KNOW, ALL MOLECULES ARE ALWAYS IN MOTION, WHETHER THEY ARE SOLID, LIQUID, OR GAS? ALL THE LITTLE MOVEMENTS OF ATOMS AND MOLECULES CREATE THERMAL ENERGY, WHICH IS WHERE HEAT COMES FROM.

IF YOU WERE TO "FREEZE" TIME, THE FIRST THING YOU WOULD NOTICE IS THAT YOU ARE LITERALLY FREEZING BECAUSE THERE IS NO MORE MOVEMENT OF MOLECULES IN THE AIR, AND THEREFORE, NO HEAT.

YOU WOULDN'T BE ABLE TO SEE BECAUSE THE WAVES THAT MAKE UP LIGHT WOULD STOP MOVING INTO YOUR EYES FOR THE CELLS IN THE RETINA, AT THE BACK OF YOUR EYE, TO ABSORB.

YOU WOULDN'T BE ABLE TO SMELL BECAUSE THE MOLECULES THAT CARRY SMELLS ARE FROZEN IN THE AIR.

YOU WOULDN'T BE ABLE TO HEAR OR SPEAK BECAUSE SOUND WAVES ARE ALSO CREATED BY MOTION— VIBRATIONS TO BE EXACT.

REMEMBER, THE AIR IS NOT EMPTY. THE AIR MOLECULES AROUND YOU WOULD BE FROZEN IN PLACE INSTEAD OF FLOWING FREELY INTO YOUR LUNGS WHEN YOU BREATHE, SO YOU WOULDN'T BE ABLE TO SUCK IN ENOUGH OXYGEN TO FUNCTION!

GASP!

OKAY, SO WHAT IF YOU DON'T REALLY "FREEZE" TIME? YOU JUST MOVE SO FAST THAT TIME HAS SLOWED DOWN. THERE ARE A FEW PROBLEMS WITH THAT, TOO.

FIRST, AS WE'VE ALREADY EXPLAINED, HEAT COMES FROM THE MOVEMENT OF MOLECULES. YOU CAN EXPERIENCE THIS FOR YOURSELF BY RUBBING YOUR HAND ON YOUR SLEEVE.
THE FRICTION (SEE PAGE 4) MAKES YOUR HAND HOT, SO MOVING AT THIS IMPOSSIBLE SPEED WOULD MAKE YOUR MUSCLES AND SKIN SUPER HOT.

YOUR BODY HEAT WOULD REACH A TEMPERATURE IMPOSSIBLE FOR A HUMAN TO SURVIVE, AND YOUR JOINTS WOULD BE RUBBING AGAINST EACH OTHER SO MUCH IT COULD CREATE PERMANENT DAMAGE.

AAAH!

OH WAIT, THAT'S RIGHT, YOU'RE A SUPERHERO WITH SUPERPOWERS. YOU CAN REGULATE YOUR BODY HEAT AND HAVE DURABLE JOINTS, OF COURSE. BUT WHAT ABOUT YOUR CLOTHES?

FINE, WE'LL GIVE YOU A SUPER SUIT THAT CAN WITHSTAND THE HEAT. NOW YOU CAN GO AND WHIZ THROUGH SOME HOMEWORK ON YOUR LAPTOP THAT IS TECHNICALLY DUE IN FIVE MINUTES, RIGHT? WELL, NO. THINK AGAIN!

IT'S SO SLOW!

WANT TO DO A LITTLE RESEARCH ON THE INTERNET? IT WON'T MOVE FAST ENOUGH FOR YOU TO USE.

WANT TO PLAY GAMES ON YOUR PHONE TO KILL TIME WHILE THE PAGE LOADS? THAT TAKES ATOMS TO MOVE AROUND AS WELL.

WANT TO DO YOUR HOMEWORK WITHOUT DOING RESEARCH? I HOPE YOUR TEACHER DOESN'T MIND A HAND-WRITTEN ESSAY, BECAUSE YOU WOULD HAVE TO WAIT FOREVER FOR YOUR COMPUTER TO REGISTER EACH SINGLE LETTER THAT YOU TYPE.

IN FACT, NOTHING ELECTRONIC WOULD WORK AT A SATISFACTORY SPEED—NO COMPUTER, NO PHONE, NO CAR—YOU COULDN'T EVEN MAKE A PIECE OF TOAST WHILE YOU WAITED ...

COME ON!

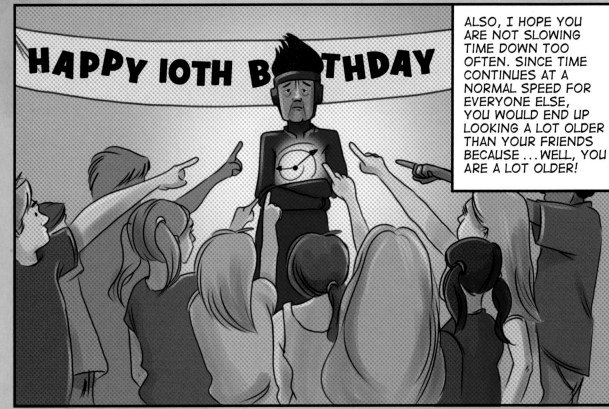

HAPPY 10TH BIRTHDAY

ALSO, I HOPE YOU ARE NOT SLOWING TIME DOWN TOO OFTEN. SINCE TIME CONTINUES AT A NORMAL SPEED FOR EVERYONE ELSE, YOU WOULD END UP LOOKING A LOT OLDER THAN YOUR FRIENDS BECAUSE ... WELL, YOU ARE A LOT OLDER!

WE MAY NEVER BE ABLE TO HAVE TIME TWISTER'S ABILITY TO FREEZE TIME, BUT WE HAVE BEEN ABLE TO CREATE MACHINES AND DEVICES THAT HAVE MADE EVERYDAY TASKS A LOT EASIER AND LESS TIME-CONSUMING. THINK ABOUT WASHING YOUR CLOTHES ...

WHAT DO YOU DO WHEN YOUR SUPERHERO SUIT NEEDS TO BE WASHED? YOU SHOVE IT INTO THE WASHING MACHINE, TURN IT ON, AND WALK OFF TO READ THIS BOOK. IF YOU HAD BEEN BORN MORE THAN TWO HUNDRED YEARS AGO, YOU WOULD HAVE HAD TO GO TO THE NEAREST RIVER OR PUMP SOME WATER INTO A TUB AND SCRUB IT BY HAND, TAKING UP A LARGE PART OF YOUR DAY!

MEGAMUSCLE: STRONGER THAN STRONG

Who wouldn't want the strength of a million people?

YOU COULD CATCH PEOPLE JUMPING OUT OF BURNING BUILDINGS WITHOUT BREAKING YOUR ARMS.

OR LIFT A 100,000 TON (100,000-TONNE) CRUISE SHIP AND CARRY IT TO SAFETY.

SO WHAT'S THE CATCH? OTHER THAN HAVING TO BE CAREFUL NOT TO BREAK EVERYTHING AND EVERYONE YOU LAY YOUR HANDS ON BECAUSE YOU CAN'T TURN OFF YOUR SUPERSTRENGTH?

MEGAMUSCLE'S SUPERPOWERS

- to have the strength of a million people
- to be able to lift anything

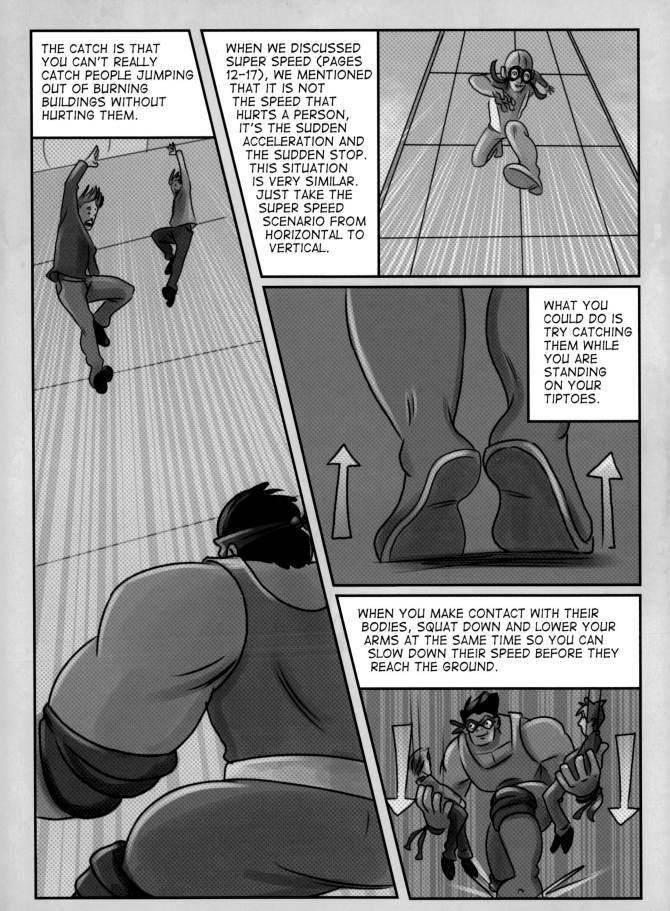

THE CATCH IS THAT YOU CAN'T REALLY CATCH PEOPLE JUMPING OUT OF BURNING BUILDINGS WITHOUT HURTING THEM.

WHEN WE DISCUSSED SUPER SPEED (PAGES 12-17), WE MENTIONED THAT IT IS NOT THE SPEED THAT HURTS A PERSON, IT'S THE SUDDEN ACCELERATION AND THE SUDDEN STOP. THIS SITUATION IS VERY SIMILAR. JUST TAKE THE SUPER SPEED SCENARIO FROM HORIZONTAL TO VERTICAL.

WHAT YOU COULD DO IS TRY CATCHING THEM WHILE YOU ARE STANDING ON YOUR TIPTOES.

WHEN YOU MAKE CONTACT WITH THEIR BODIES, SQUAT DOWN AND LOWER YOUR ARMS AT THE SAME TIME SO YOU CAN SLOW DOWN THEIR SPEED BEFORE THEY REACH THE GROUND.

BUT EVEN THEN, WHETHER YOU CAN SAVE THEM OR NOT DEPENDS ON THE HEIGHT THEY ARE FALLING FROM. FROM THE HEIGHT OF FIVE FLOORS, A FREE-FALLING PERSON WOULD REACH THE SPEED OF APPROXIMATELY 40 MPH (65 KPH) BY THE TIME OF IMPACT, AND MOST PEOPLE WOULD NOT SURVIVE THAT.

SURVIVAL RATE DROPS TO ALMOST ZERO PERCENT WHEN YOU INCREASE THE HEIGHT TO EIGHT FLOORS, WHICH WOULD LEAD TO A SPEED OF 50 MPH (80 KPH) BY THE TIME OF IMPACT. THIS IS WHY RESCUE AIR CUSHIONS WERE INVENTED. EVERY GOOD SUPERHERO SHOULD CARRY ONE WITH HIM OR HER.

A RESCUE AIR CUSHION IS LIKE A GIANT WHOOPEE CUSHION, WHICH IS BASICALLY AN AIR MATTRESS WITH A HOLE ON THE SIDE. WHEN A PERSON FALLS INTO IT, IT ABSORBS THE SHOCK OF THE FALL AS AIR IS RAPIDLY SQUEEZED OUT OF THE CUSHION. USED CORRECTLY, THE PERSON DECELERATES AT A REDUCED RATE AND SURVIVES.

OKAY, SO YOUR SUPERSTRENGTH WOULD NOT BE VERY USEFUL IN THAT SITUATION, BUT WHAT ABOUT LIFTING GIANT THINGS LIKE A CRUISE SHIP OR AN AIRPLANE?

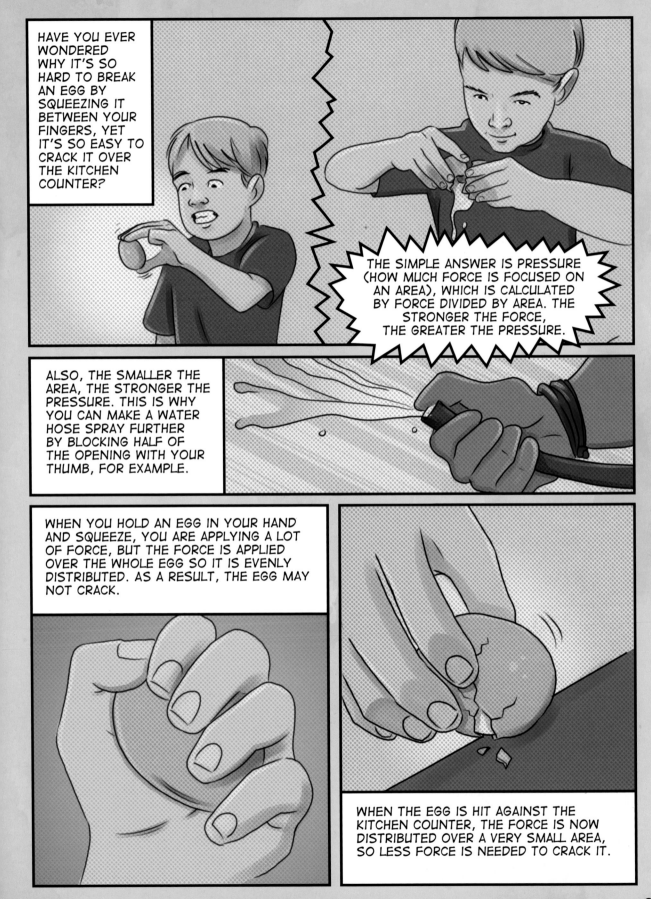

HAVE YOU EVER WONDERED WHY IT'S SO HARD TO BREAK AN EGG BY SQUEEZING IT BETWEEN YOUR FINGERS, YET IT'S SO EASY TO CRACK IT OVER THE KITCHEN COUNTER?

THE SIMPLE ANSWER IS PRESSURE (HOW MUCH FORCE IS FOCUSED ON AN AREA), WHICH IS CALCULATED BY FORCE DIVIDED BY AREA. THE STRONGER THE FORCE, THE GREATER THE PRESSURE.

ALSO, THE SMALLER THE AREA, THE STRONGER THE PRESSURE. THIS IS WHY YOU CAN MAKE A WATER HOSE SPRAY FURTHER BY BLOCKING HALF OF THE OPENING WITH YOUR THUMB, FOR EXAMPLE.

WHEN YOU HOLD AN EGG IN YOUR HAND AND SQUEEZE, YOU ARE APPLYING A LOT OF FORCE, BUT THE FORCE IS APPLIED OVER THE WHOLE EGG SO IT IS EVENLY DISTRIBUTED. AS A RESULT, THE EGG MAY NOT CRACK.

WHEN THE EGG IS HIT AGAINST THE KITCHEN COUNTER, THE FORCE IS NOW DISTRIBUTED OVER A VERY SMALL AREA, SO LESS FORCE IS NEEDED TO CRACK IT.

THIS IS ALSO WHY WE CAN CARRY VERY HEAVY BACKPACKS AND WALK AROUND ALL DAY WITH THEM, YET A LITTLE THUMBTACK CAN PIERCE OUR SKIN.

OUCH!

IF WE APPLY THIS PRINCIPLE TO LIFTING A GIANT THING LIKE A CRUISE SHIP WITH YOUR HANDS, THE QUESTION IS NOT WHETHER YOU ARE STRONG ENOUGH TO DO IT OR NOT, IT'S WHETHER THE CRUISE SHIP IS STRONG ENOUGH TO BE LIFTED BY YOU!

OOPS!

YOU ARE MORE LIKELY TO PIERCE WHATEVER GIANT OBJECT IT IS YOU ARE LIFTING THAN TO ACTUALLY LIFT IT. THINK OF YOURSELF AS THE SMALL SURFACE OF A PIN PUTTING PRESSURE ON THE LARGER OBJECT.

IT SOUNDS LIKE BEING SUPER STRONG IS MORE LIKELY TO CAUSE DESTRUCTION THAN ACTUALLY BE OF USE...BUT HAVE YOU EVER HEARD STORIES OF ORDINARY PEOPLE LIFTING CARS IN ORDER TO SAVE THEIR FAMILY? THAT CAN HAPPEN WHEN A LARGE AMOUNT OF ADRENALINE KICKS IN.

ADRENALINE IS A HORMONE THAT YOUR BODY RELEASES, ESPECIALLY IN STRESSFUL SITUATIONS. ADRENALINE INCREASES YOUR BLOOD CIRCULATION AND PREPARES YOUR MUSCLES FOR PHYSICAL EFFORT.

OUR MUSCLE FIBERS ARE ACTUALLY PHYSICALLY CAPABLE OF ALLOWING US TO LIFT AN UNREASONABLE AMOUNT OF WEIGHT IN A MOMENT OF CRISIS. THE KEY WORD HERE IS "MOMENT."

BECAUSE OUR TENDONS AND JOINTS ARE NOT BUILT TO ENDURE THAT KIND OF STRESS ALL THE TIME, OUR BRAIN LIMITS OUR ABILITIES IN ORDER TO KEEP US FROM HARMING OURSELVES. BUT IT'S ALWAYS GOOD TO KNOW THAT, WHEN NEEDED, WE CAN ALL BE SUPERHEROES!

GLOSSARY

acceleration A MEASUREMENT OF HOW QUICKLY THE SPEED OF A MOVING OBJECT IS INCREASING

adrenaline A HORMONE (CHEMICAL SUBSTANCE) PRODUCED BY THE BODY WHEN A PERSON IS FRIGHTENED, ANGRY, OR EXCITED, WHICH MAKES THE HEART BEAT FASTER AND PREPARES THE BODY TO REACT TO DANGER

atoms THE BUILDING BLOCKS OF MATTER

core THE CENTRAL OR MOST IMPORTANT PART OF SOMETHING

durable ABLE TO WITHSTAND WEAR, PRESSURE, OR DAMAGE

expansion THE ACTION OF BECOMING LARGER OR GROWING IN SIZE

force A PUSH, PULL, OR INFLUENCE ON AN OBJECT

friction A FORCE THAT SLOWS DOWN OBJECTS AS THEY SLIDE OR SCRAPE AGAINST EACH OTHER

gas MATTER THAT HAS NO DEFINITE SIZE OR SHAPE BECAUSE THE MOLECULES THAT CONSTITUTE IT ARE MOVING FAST AND ARE WIDELY SPREAD OUT. ONE OF THE THREE MAIN STATES OF MATTER

gravity A PULLING FORCE THAT ATTRACTS OBJECTS TOGETHER. IT USUALLY REFERS TO THE FORCE PULLING EVERYTHING TOWARD THE CENTER OF THE EARTH

hypothermia THE CONDITION OF HAVING A DANGEROUSLY LOW BODY TEMPERATURE

inertia THE TENDENCY OF AN OBJECT THAT IS NOT MOVING TO REMAIN STILL, OR OF AN OBJECT THAT IS MOVING TO CONTINUE TO MOVE, UNLESS SOMETHING ELSE MOVES OR STOPS THE OBJECT

liquid MATTER THAT HAS A DEFINITE SIZE BUT NO DEFINITE SHAPE BECAUSE THE ATOMS THAT CONSTITUTE IT ARE LOOSELY LINKED. ONE OF THE THREE MAIN STATES OF MATTER

mass THE AMOUNT OF MATTER IN AN OBJECT

matter ANYTHING THAT HAS MASS AND TAKES UP SPACE, IT IS THE STUFF THAT ALL OBJECTS AND MATERIALS AROUND US ARE MADE OF

molecules UNITS OF MATTER MADE OF ATOMS BONDED TOGETHER

motion THE ACTION OR PROCESS OF MOVING OR BEING MOVED

perception THE ABILITY TO BECOME AWARE OF SOMETHING THROUGH THE SENSES

pressure A WAY OF MEASURING HOW MUCH FORCE IS ACTING OVER AN AREA

regulate TO CONTROL SOMETHING, ESPECIALLY BY MAKING IT WORK IN A PARTICULAR WAY

retina THE AREA AT THE BACK OF THE EYE THAT RECEIVES LIGHT AND SENDS PICTURES OF WHAT THE EYE SEES TO THE BRAIN

slingshot A Y-SHAPED STICK OR PIECE OF METAL WITH A PIECE OF ELASTIC ATTACHED TO THE TOP PARTS, USED ESPECIALLY BY CHILDREN FOR SHOOTING SMALL PEBBLES, STONES, OR ROCKS

solid MATTER THAT HAS A DEFINITE SIZE AND SHAPE BECAUSE THE ATOMS THAT CONSTITUTE IT ARE TIGHTLY PACKED. ONE OF THE THREE MAIN STATES OF MATTER

speed HOW FAR AN OBJECT MOVES IN A GIVEN TIME

thermal RELATED TO HEAT

velocity THE SPEED OF SOMETHING IN A GIVEN DIRECTION

vibration THE INSTANCE OF MOVING BACK AND FORTH VERY RAPIDLY AND STEADILY

volume THE AMOUNT OF SPACE SOMETHING TAKES UP

weight THE FORCE CAUSED BY GRAVITY AND MEASURED IN NEWTONS. THE WEIGHT OF AN OBJECT IS HOW HARD GRAVITY PULLS DOWN ON IT

FURTHER INFORMATION

WEBSITES

www.dkfindout.com/uk/science/forces-and-motion/
INFORMATION AND QUIZZES ABOUT FORCES AND MOTION

www.physics4kids.com/files/motion_intro.html
A WEBSITE THAT EXPLAINS FORCES AND MOTION IN MORE DEPTH

idahoptv.org/sciencetrek/topics/force_and_motion/index.cfm
VIDEOS, GAMES, AND FACTS ABOUT FORCES AND MOTION

https://ed.ted.com/series/?series=superhero-science
AUTHOR JOY LIN'S TED ED VIDEOS ABOUT SCIENCE AND SUPERHEROES

https://www.khanacademy.org/science/physics/forces-newtons-laws
A TEACHING WEBSITE THAT EXPLAINS FORCES AND NEWTON'S
LAWS OF MOTION, ALSO INCLUDES QUIZZES

BOOKS

Mind Webs: Forces and Motion BY ANNA CLAYBOURNE (WAYLAND, 2014)

Science is Everywhere: Forces in Action
BY ROB COLSON (FRANKLIN WATTS, 2017)

Science Makers: Making with Forces
BY ANNA CLAYBOURNE (WAYLAND, 2018)

**Graphic Science: A Crash Course in Forces and
Motion with Max Axiom, Super Scientist**
BY EMILY SOHN AND CHARLES BARNETT III (CAPSTONE PRESS, 2017)

EVERY EFFORT HAS BEEN MADE BY THE PUBLISHERS TO ENSURE THAT
THE WEBSITES IN THIS BOOK ARE SUITABLE FOR CHILDREN, THAT THEY
ARE OF THE HIGHEST EDUCATIONAL VALUE, AND THAT THEY CONTAIN
NO INAPPROPRIATE OR OFFENSIVE MATERIAL. HOWEVER, BECAUSE OF
THE NATURE OF THE INTERNET, IT IS IMPOSSIBLE TO GUARANTEE THAT
THE CONTENTS OF THESE SITES WILL NOT BE ALTERED. WE STRONGLY
ADVISE THAT INTERNET ACCESS IS SUPERVISED BY A RESPONSIBLE ADULT.

INDEX